The Winemaker's RECORD BOOK

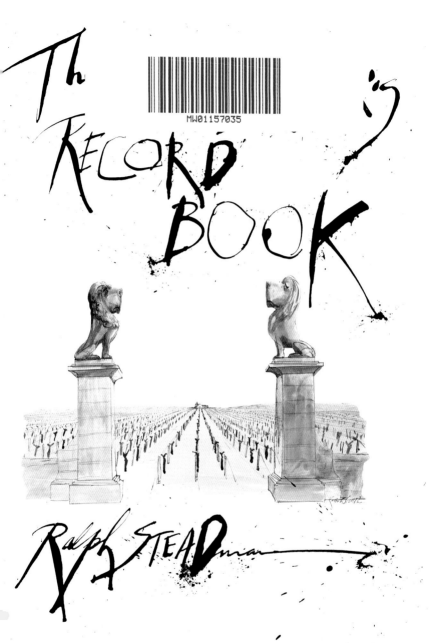

Ralph STEADman

THE WINE APPRECIATION GUILD

Pubished in the United States, 2001
by The Wine Appreciation Guild Ltd,
360 Swift Avenue, South San Francisco CA 94080, 800 231-9463

First published in the United Kingdom in 1994 by
Ebury Press Stationery
Random House, 20 Vauxhall Bridge Road, London SW1V 2SA
Random House UK Limited Reg. No. 954009

5 7 9 10 8 6

Set in Berling by SX Composing Ltd, Rayleigh, Essex
Printed and bound in Malaysia
Designed by David Fordham

Ebury Press Stationery would like to acknowledge
the cooperation of Oddbins for the use of illustrations in this book.

Introduction

EVERY BOTTLE TELLS A STORY BUT IF YOU DON'T MAKE A note of it you will forget. Forget it by all means if it is a rotten story, but occasionally like a good joke you want to remember, know it well enough to recall, and relive it even if you have to pay for it.

Bottles of wine consumed represent moments shared, good and bad, and it has to be said, the finest wines have sometimes been shot on the worst company. If you drink alone you talk to the bottle and the conversation can be second to none or a blizzard of maudlin drivel. Either way you want to do it again or avoid it.

If your memory is like mine, you can't, because you have forgotten what it was that helped you to reach Nirvana or Purgatory. The compulsion to repeat is common to all, and there is a basic desire to keep the information in an accessible place in order to do so. An Off-Licence can be a minefield of dangerous choices and promising labels, but if you have your little book with you, you can whip it out and enquire with a certain élan, 'what was that spicy little Gewürztraminer you sold me last Tuesday? An Altenberg de Bergheim, was it not? It saw the fish off eloquently and the Bishop got quite silly, etc.'

The Wine Buyer's Record Book can be just such a useful ready reckoner, limited only by your own discretion and zeal. It is not a puerile filofax of grey business meetings and defunct addresses, but a rich diary of golden moments, succinctly recorded in your own timeless shorthand to recall a bewitched bottle that worked indescribable magic and uncontrolled desires – and just when you thought you were going to have an early night. . . .

Ralph STEADMAN:

Vintage Chart

WINES

YEAR

2000										
1999										
1998										
1997										
1996										
1995										
1994										
1993										
1992										
1991										
1990										
1989										
1988										
1987										
1986										
1985										
1984										
1983										
1982										
1981										
1980										

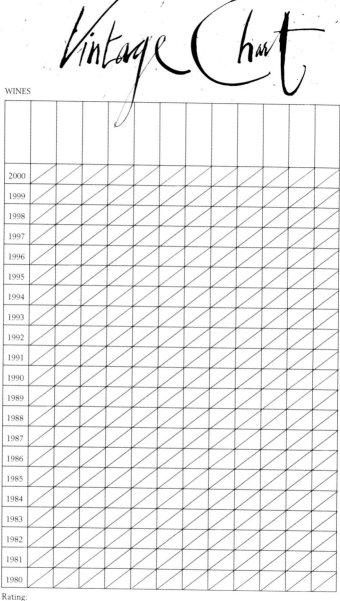

Rating:
6 = Outstanding
5 = Very good, some outstanding wines
4 = An average year, some good wines
but variable

3 = Sound but unexciting
2 = A poor year
1 = Very poor

L = To lay down
M = Maybe drink now
N = Drink now
D = Past their best

e.g. [4 / M]

The REDS

DATE	SUPPLIER	NAME · VINTNER · REGION

YEAR	PRICE	COMMENTS	RATING	★

DATE	SUPPLIER	NAME · VINTNER · REGION

YEAR	PRICE	COMMENTS	RATING	★

DATE	SUPPLIER	NAME · VINTNER · REGION

YEAR	PRICE	COMMENTS	RATING	★

DATE	SUPPLIER	NAME · VINTNER · REGION

A BERET of BASQUES

YEAR	PRICE	COMMENTS	RATING	★

Ralph STEADman

DATE	SUPPLIER	NAME · VINTNER · REGION

YEAR	PRICE	COMMENTS	RATING	★

DATE	SUPPLIER	NAME · VINTNER · REGION

YEAR	PRICE	COMMENTS	RATING	★

DATE	SUPPLIER	NAME · VINTNER · REGION

YEAR	PRICE	COMMENTS	RATING	★

Recommendation

SUPPLIER	NAME · VINTNER	YEAR	PRICE

The WHITES

The Dry WHITE

DATE	SUPPLIER	NAME · VINTNER · REGION

YEAR	PRICE	COMMENTS	RATING	★

DATE	SUPPLIER	NAME · VINTNER · REGION

YEAR	PRICE	COMMENTS	RATING	★

DATE	SUPPLIER	NAME · VINTNER · REGION

YEAR	PRICE	COMMENTS	RATING	★

DATE	SUPPLIER	NAME · VINTNER · REGION

YEAR	PRICE	COMMENTS	RATING	★

DATE	SUPPLIER	NAME · VINTNER · REGION

YEAR	PRICE	COMMENTS	RATING	★

Recommendation

SUPPLIER	NAME · VINTNER	YEAR	PRICE

The ROSÉ

The Chancellor of the Wine Guild
Lord Montagu ——— a brace of Wine Experts.

DATE	SUPPLIER	NAME · VINTNER · REGION

YEAR	PRICE	COMMENTS	RATING	★

DATE	SUPPLIER	NAME · VINTNER · REGION

YEAR	PRICE	COMMENTS	RATING	★

DATE	SUPPLIER	NAME · VINTNER · REGION

YEAR	PRICE	COMMENTS	RATING	★

Recommendation

SUPPLIER	NAME · VINTNER	YEAR	PRICE

The BUBBLIES

GUY DEVAUX - High Priest of Sparkling WINE   Ralph Steadman

DATE	SUPPLIER	NAME · VINTNER · REGION

YEAR	PRICE	COMMENTS	RATING	★

DATE	SUPPLIER	NAME · VINTNER · REGION

YEAR	PRICE	COMMENTS	RATING	★

DATE	SUPPLIER	NAME · VINTNER · REGION

YEAR	PRICE	COMMENTS	RATING	★

Recommendation

SUPPLIER	NAME · VINTNER	YEAR	PRICE

The PORTS

THE LISTING TO PORT.

DATE	SUPPLIER	NAME · VINTNER · REGION

YEAR	PRICE	COMMENTS	RATING	★

DATE	SUPPLIER	NAME · VINTNER · REGION

YEAR	PRICE	COMMENTS	RATING	★

SANDEMAN

DATE	SUPPLIER	NAME · VINTNER · REGION

YEAR	PRICE	COMMENTS	RATING	★

Recommendation

SUPPLIER	NAME · VINTNER	YEAR	PRICE

The LAYING DOWN

DATE	SUPPLIER	NAME · VINTNER · REGION

YEAR	PRICE	COMMENTS	READY

DATE	SUPPLIER	NAME · VINTNER · REGION

YEAR	PRICE	COMMENTS	READY

SUPPLIER	NAME · VINTNER	TEL/FAX

SUPPLIER	ADDRESS	TEL/FAX